ISBN- 13: 978 1542618472

Printed in The United States of America

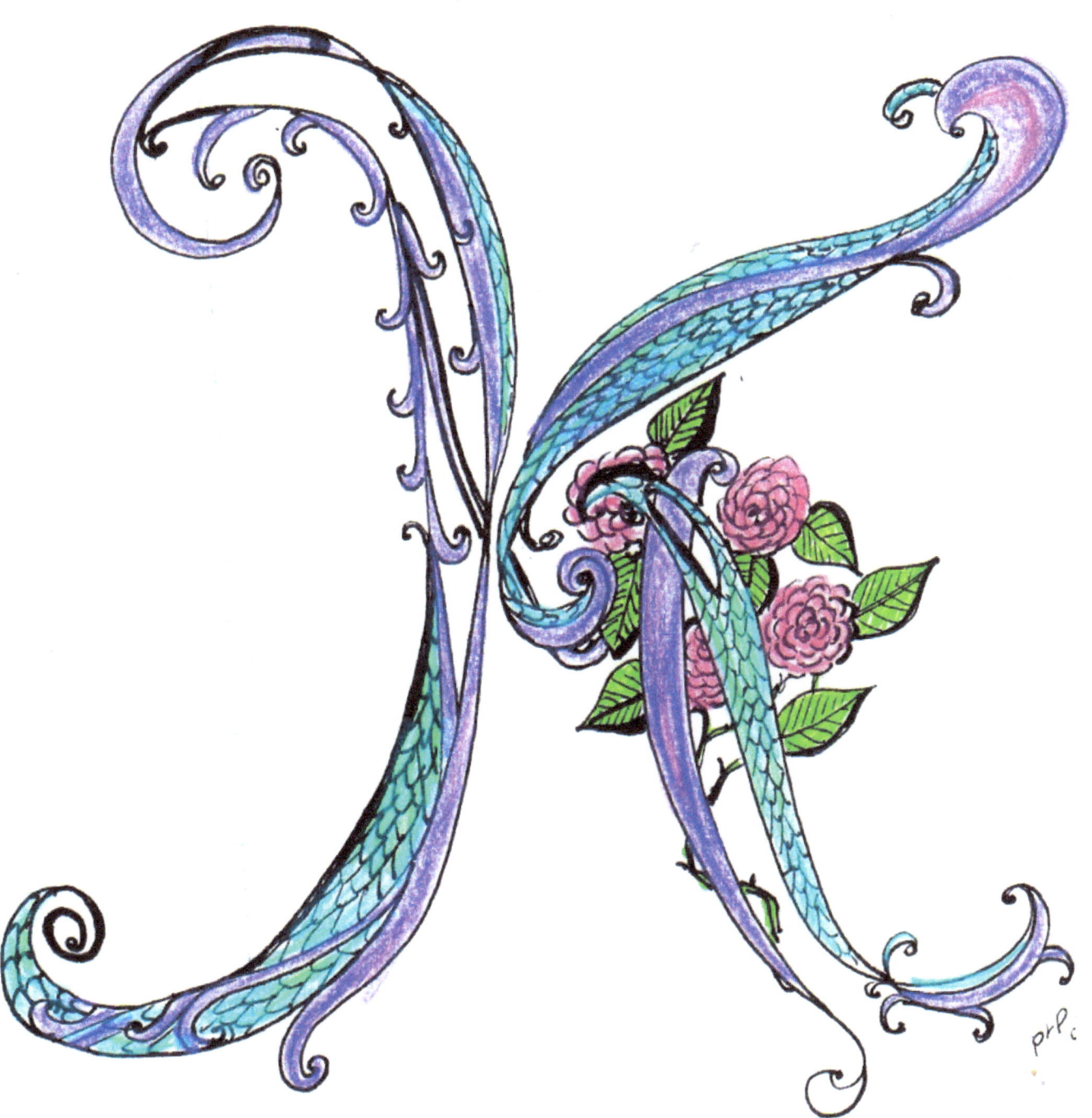

The Kingdom Letter K

Coloring Book

By Peggy Louise Parrish
C. 2017

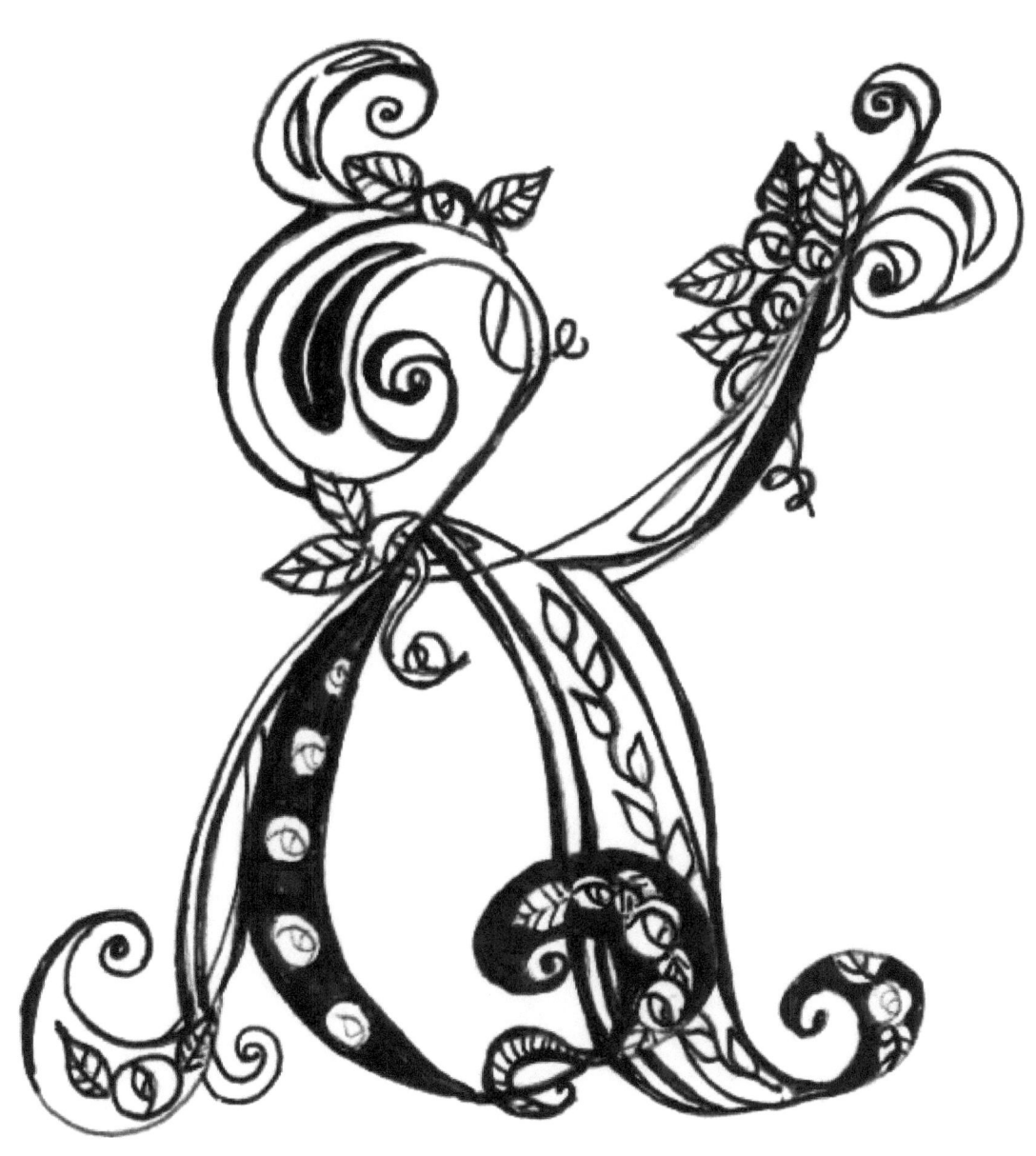

PLP c.

9

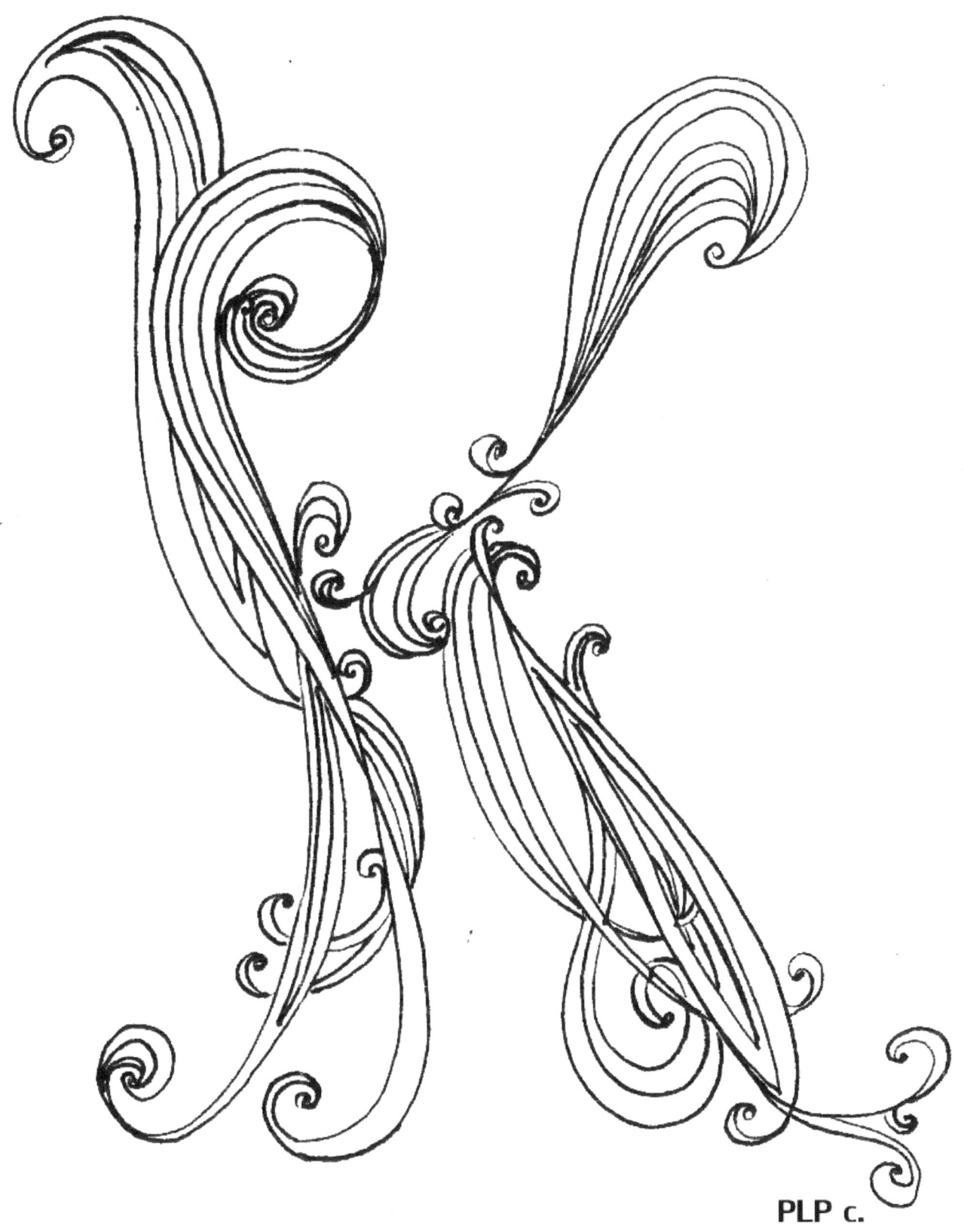

PLP c.

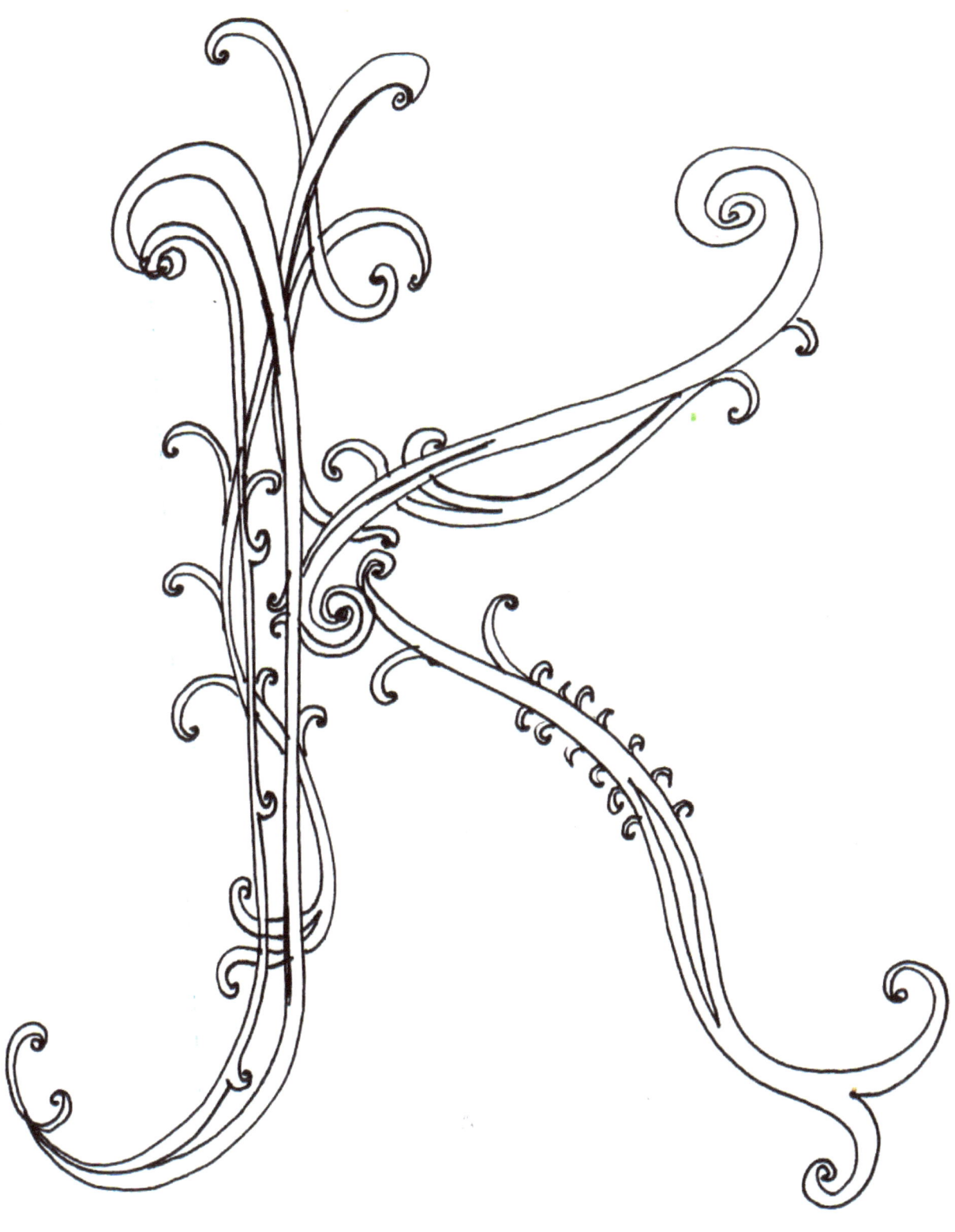

PLP c.

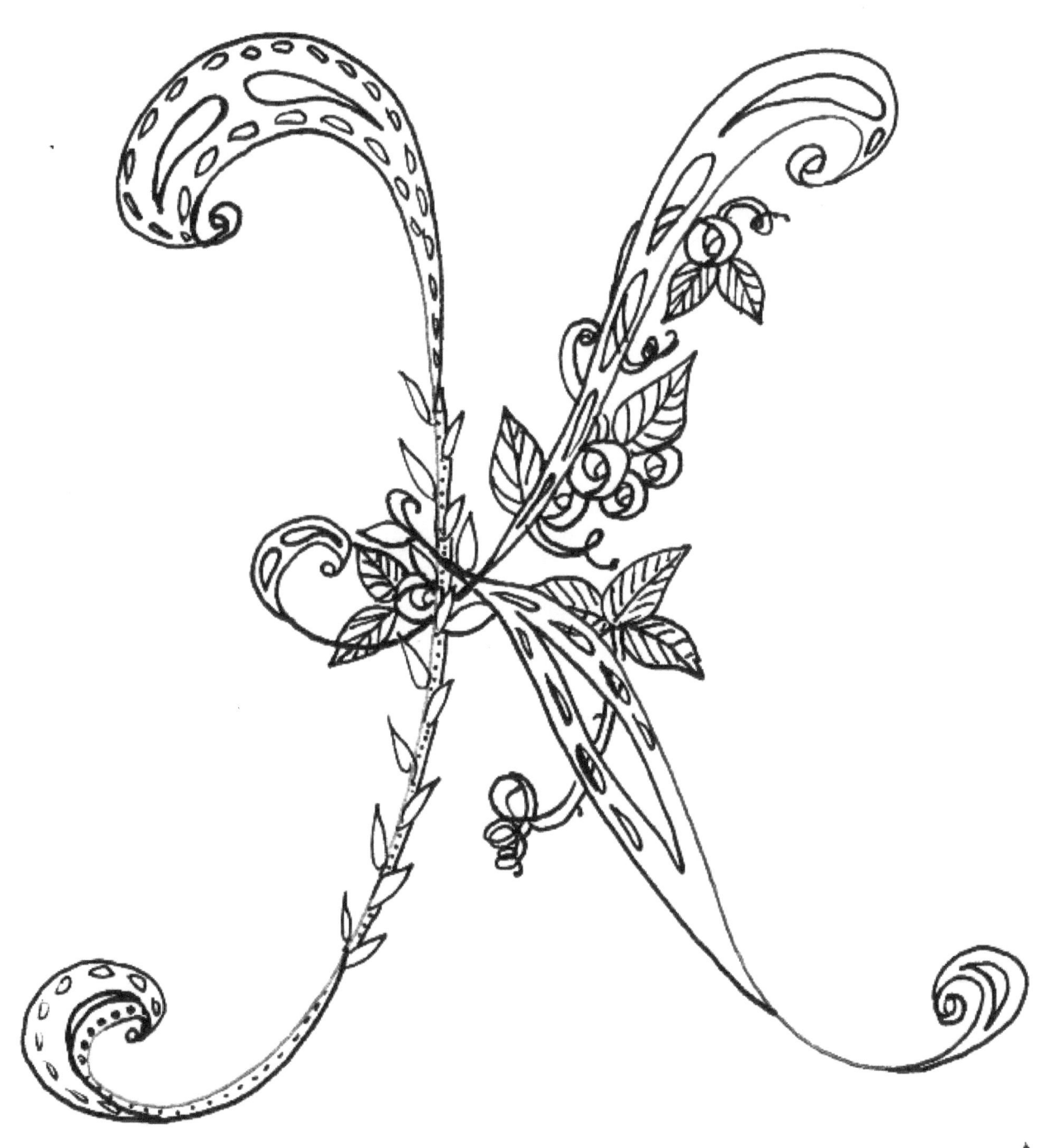

PdPd 2010

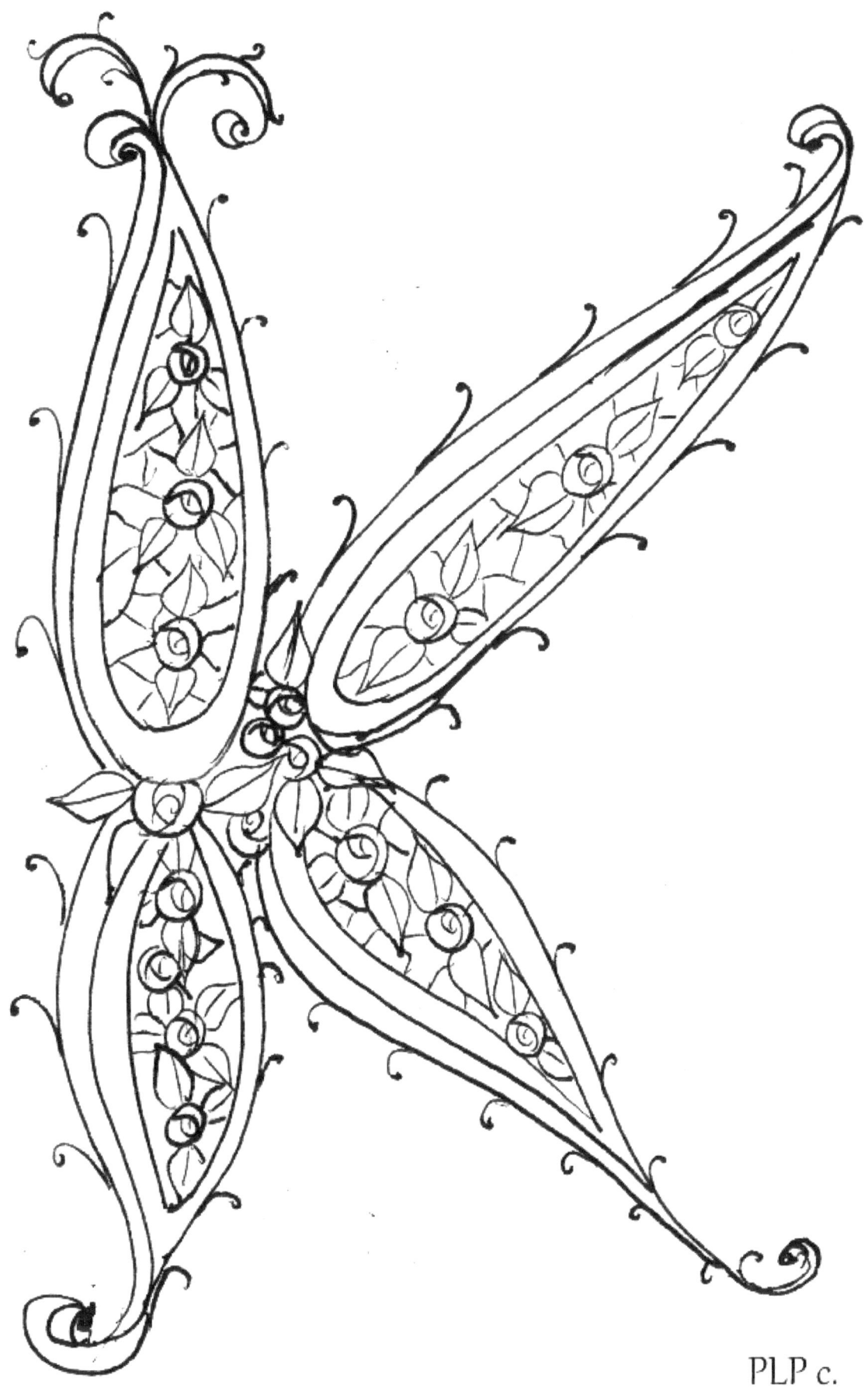

PLP c.

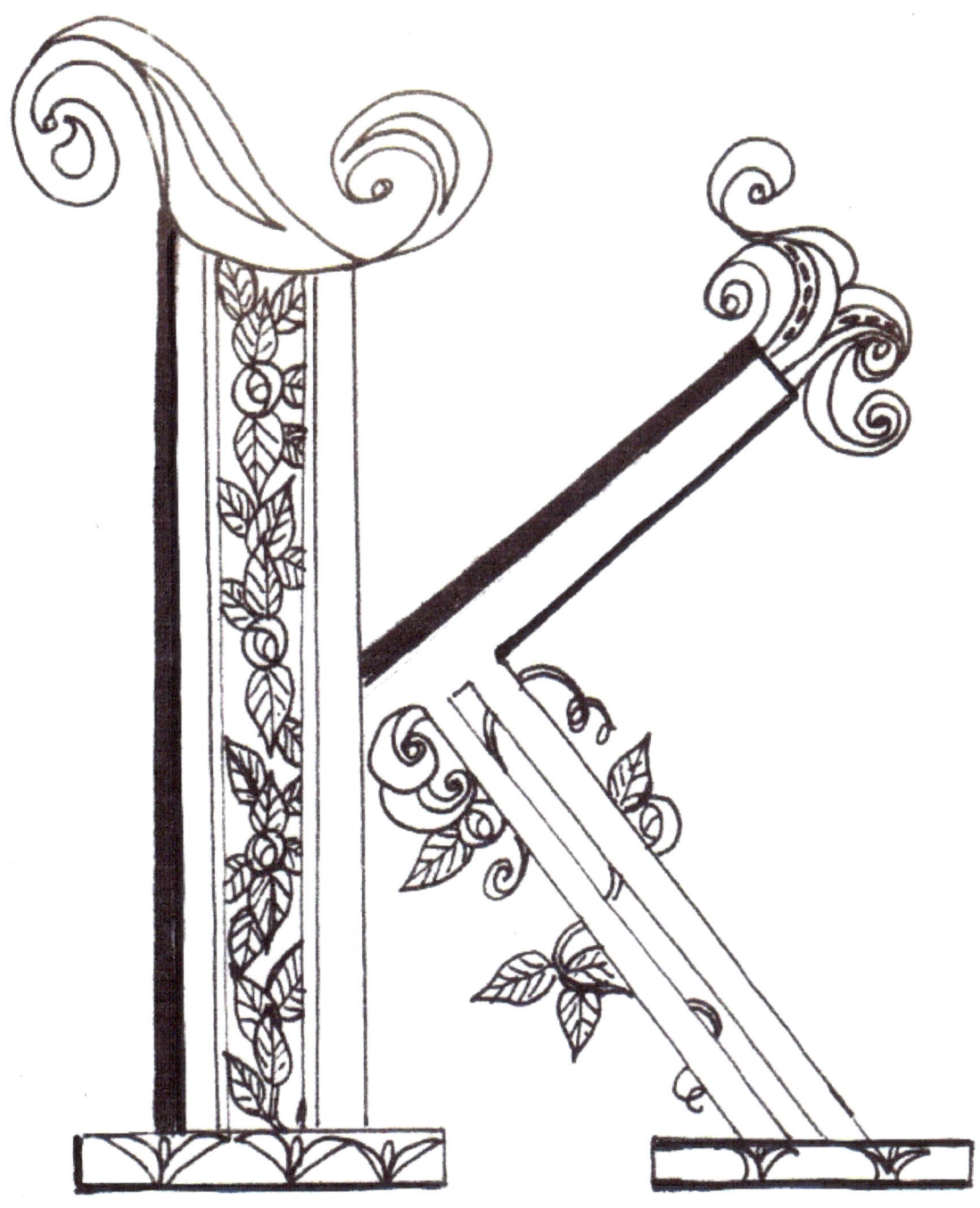

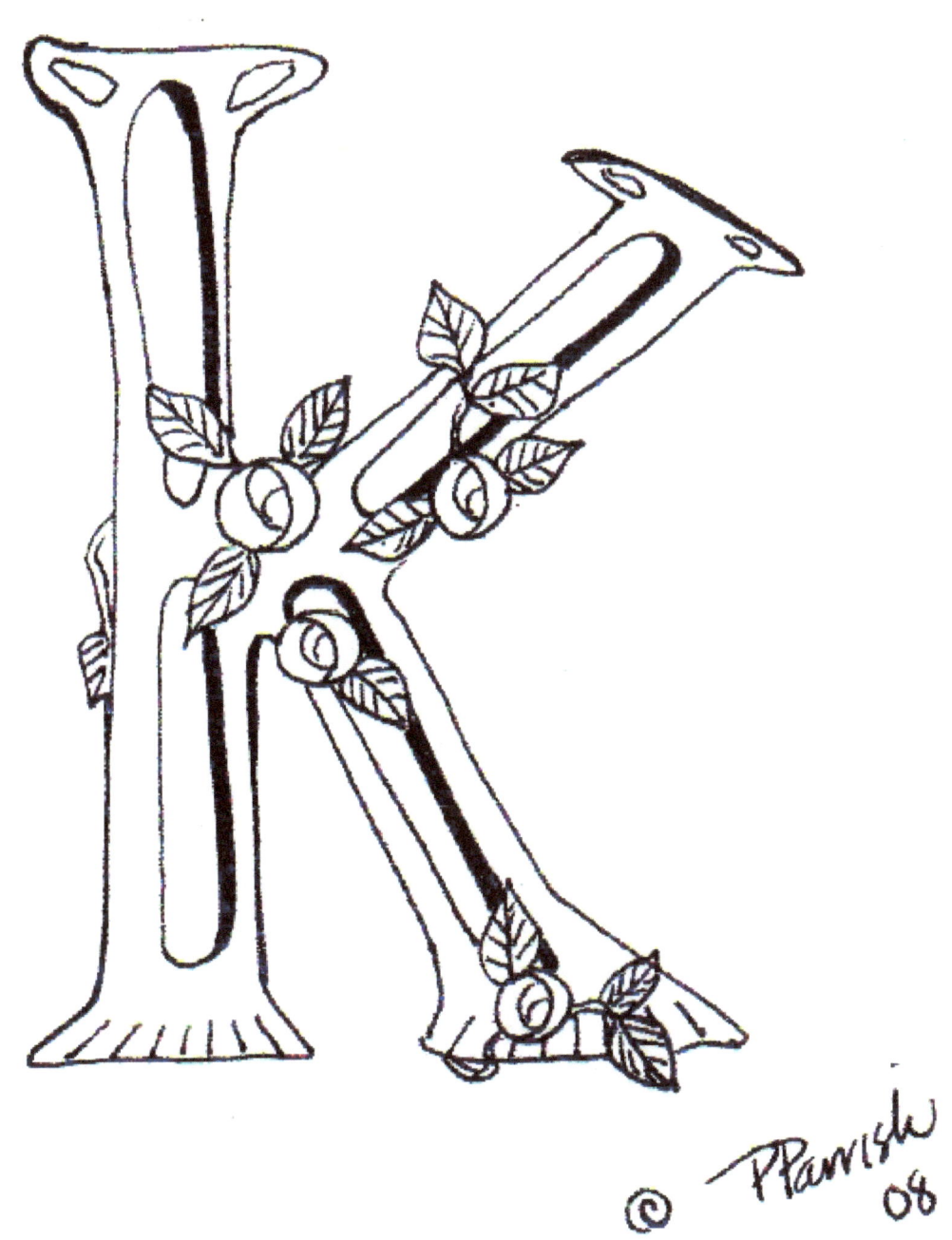

PLP c.

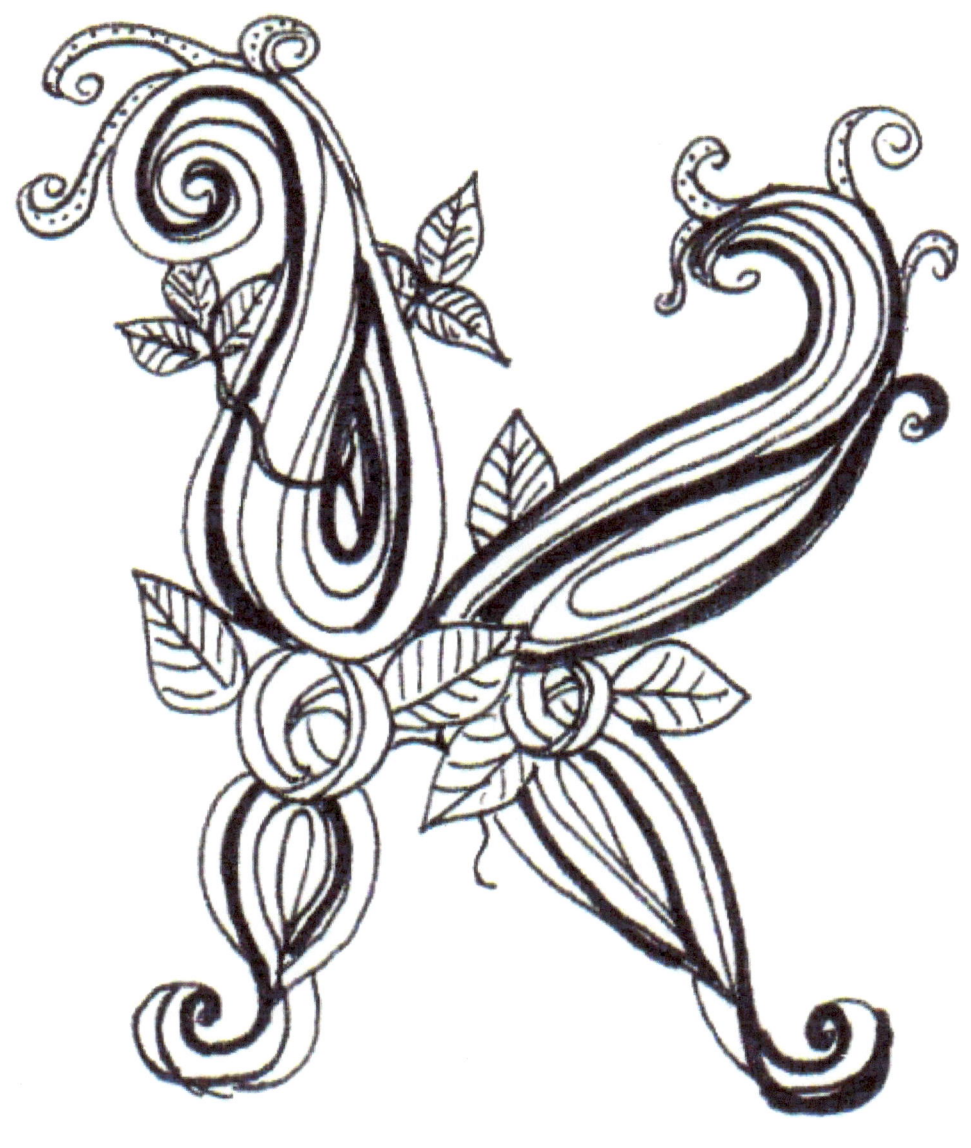

PLP c.

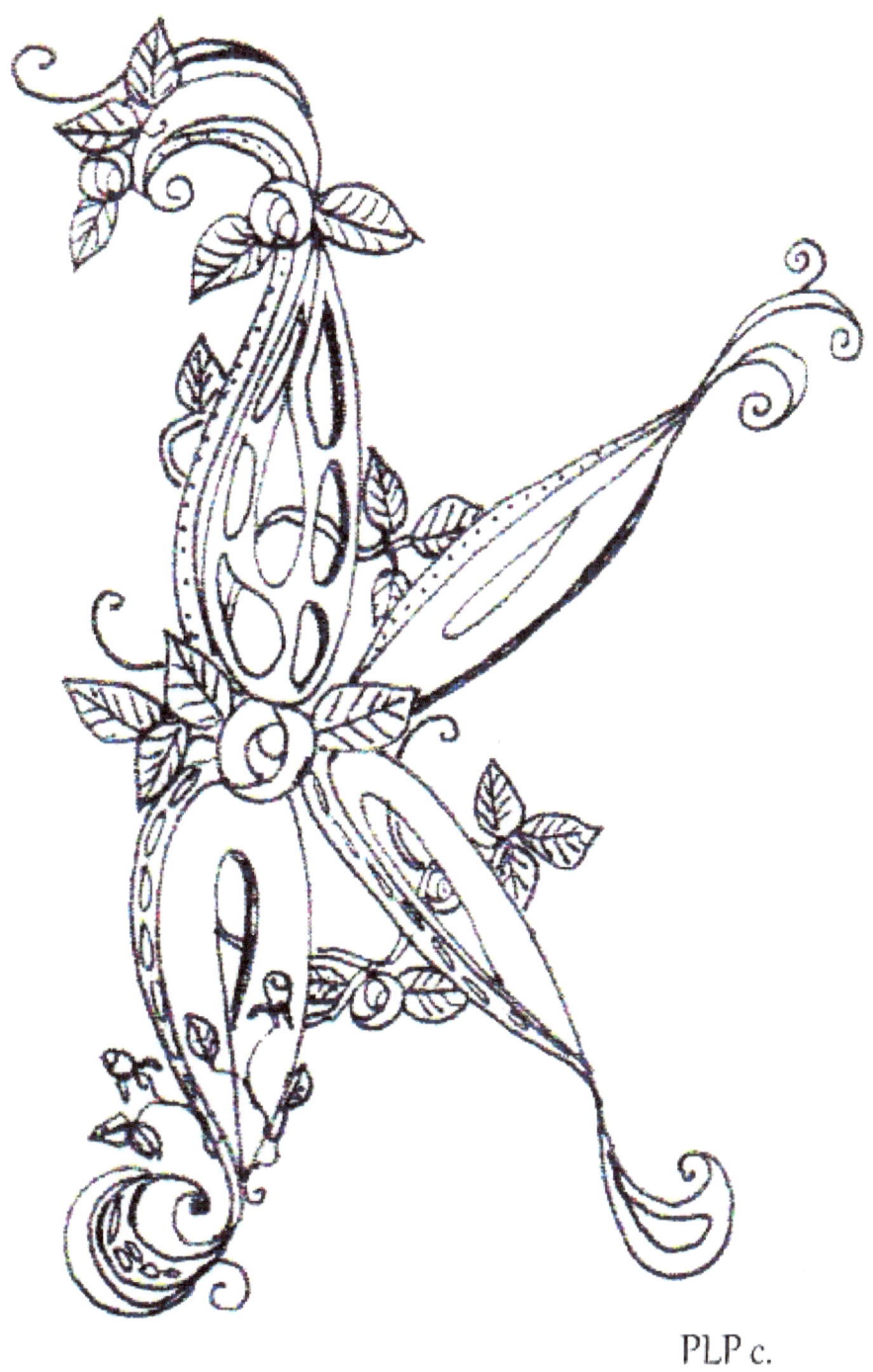

PLP c.

PLP c.

29

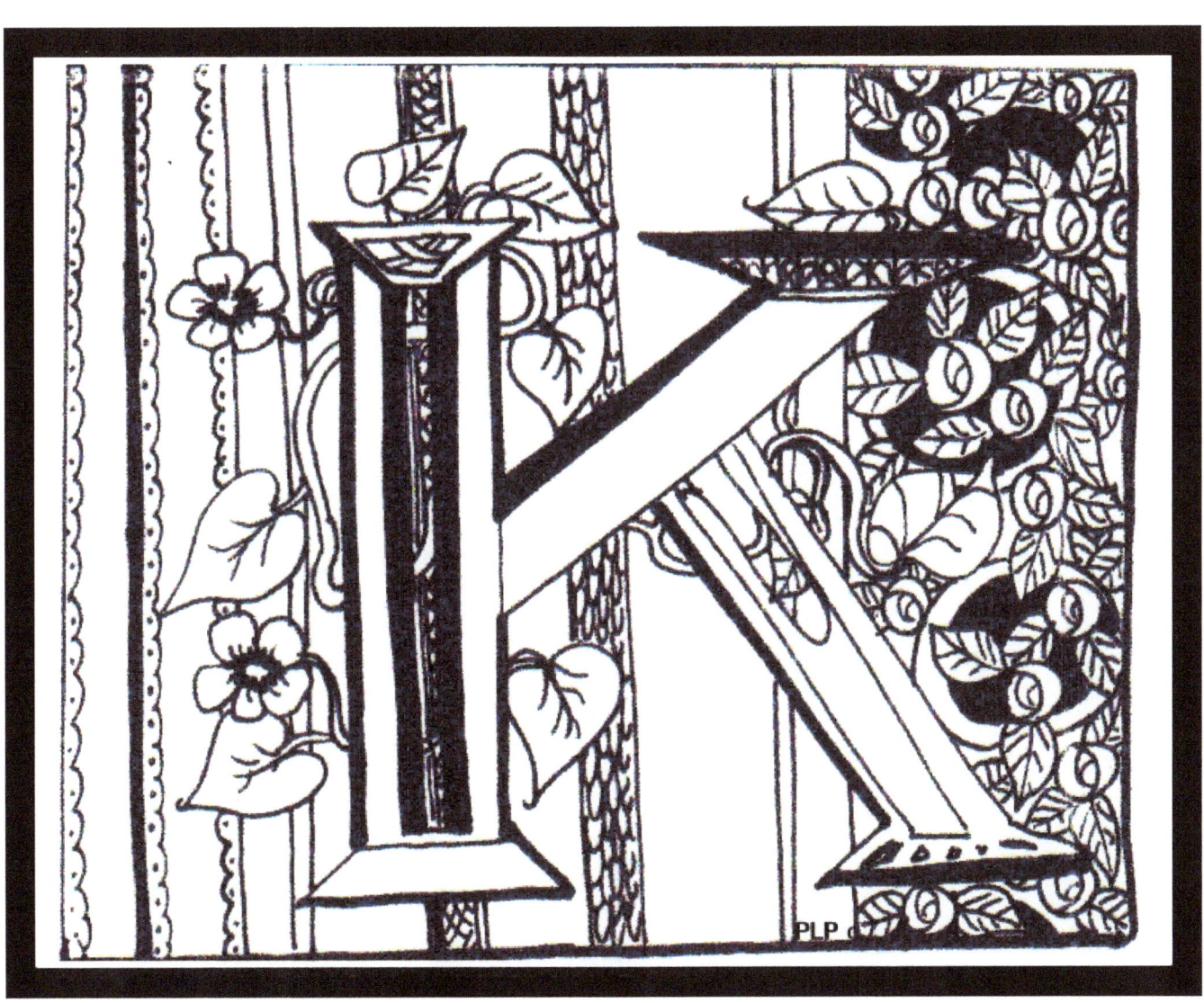

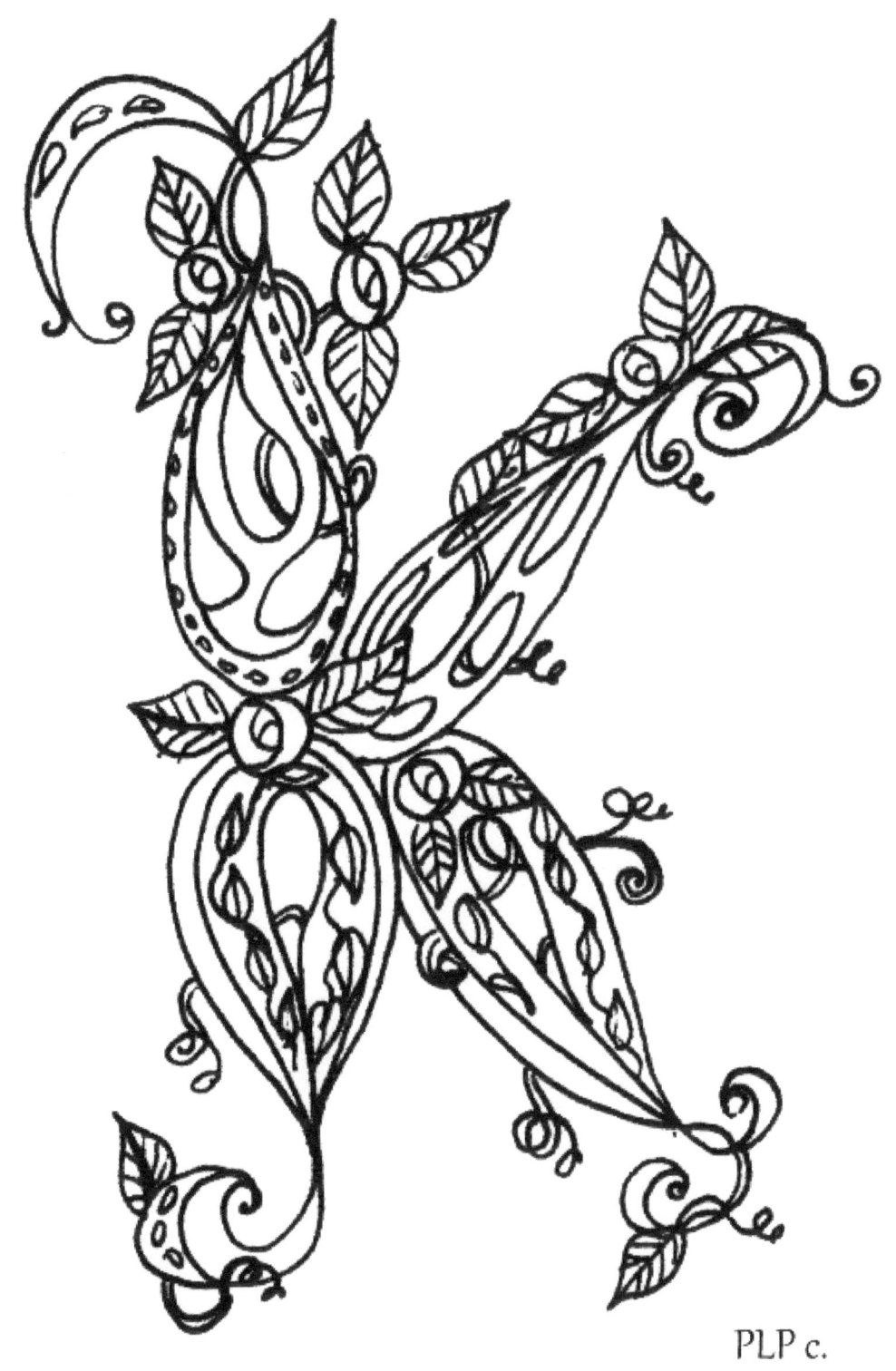

PLP c.

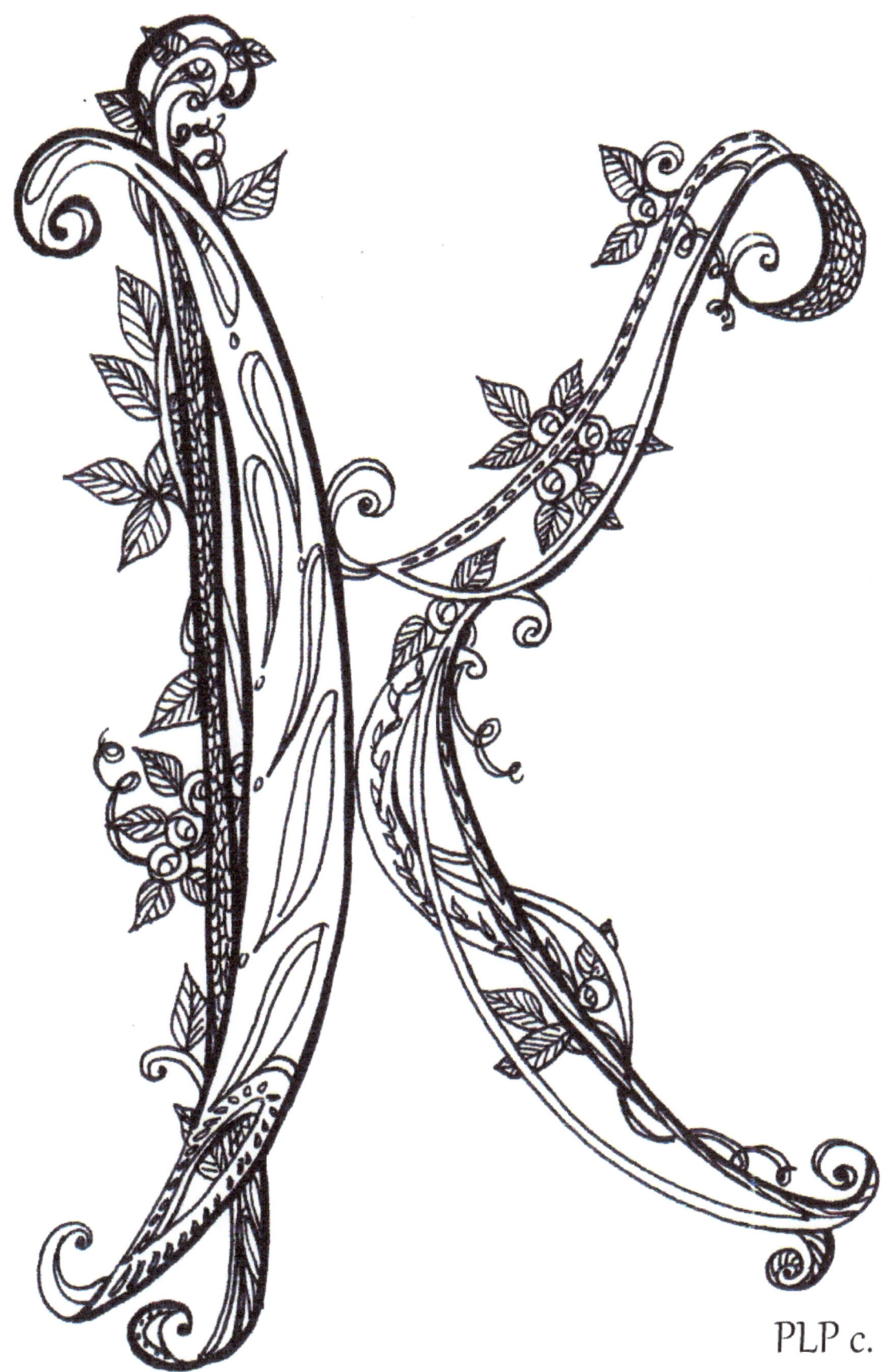

PLP c.

35

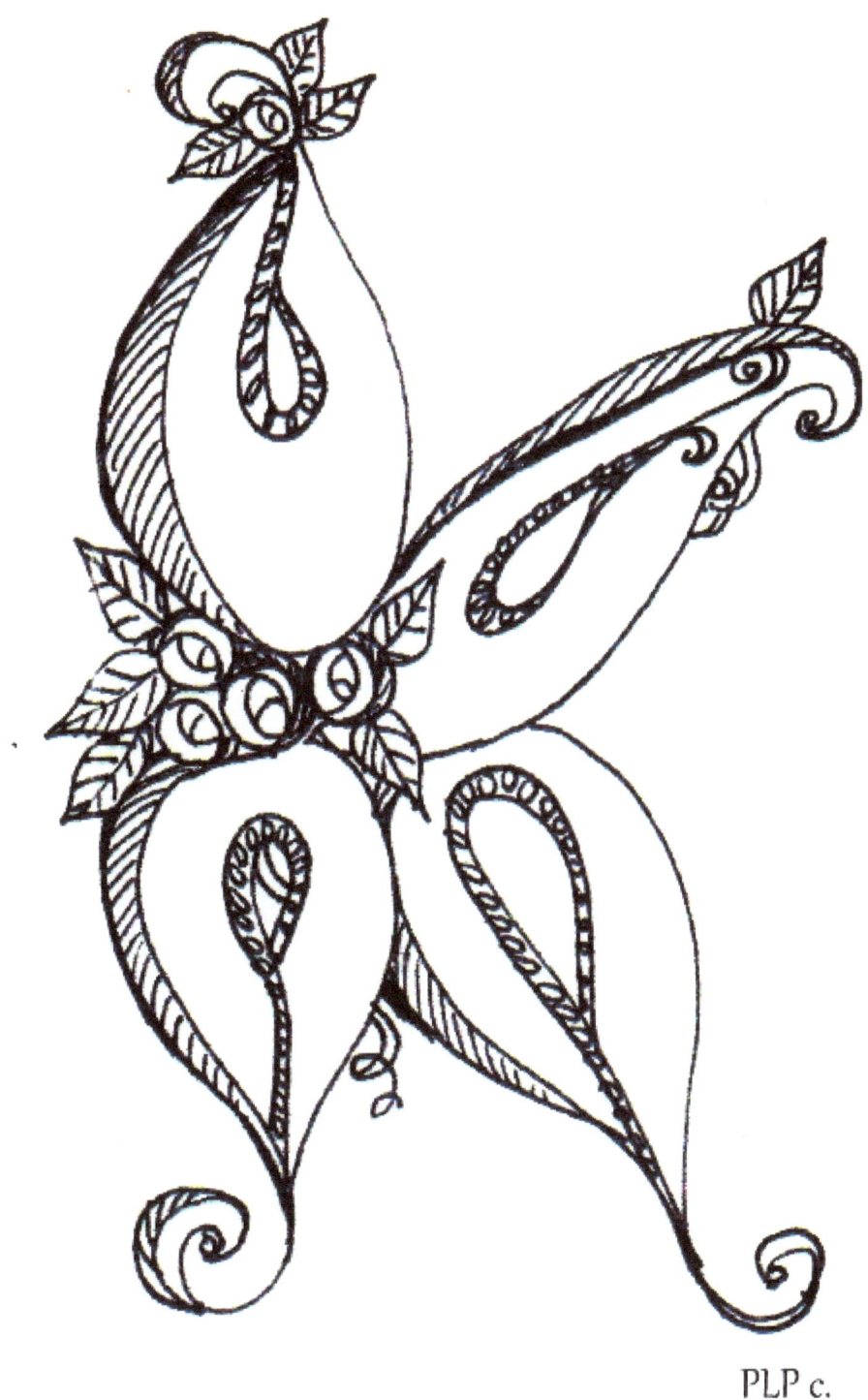

PLP c.

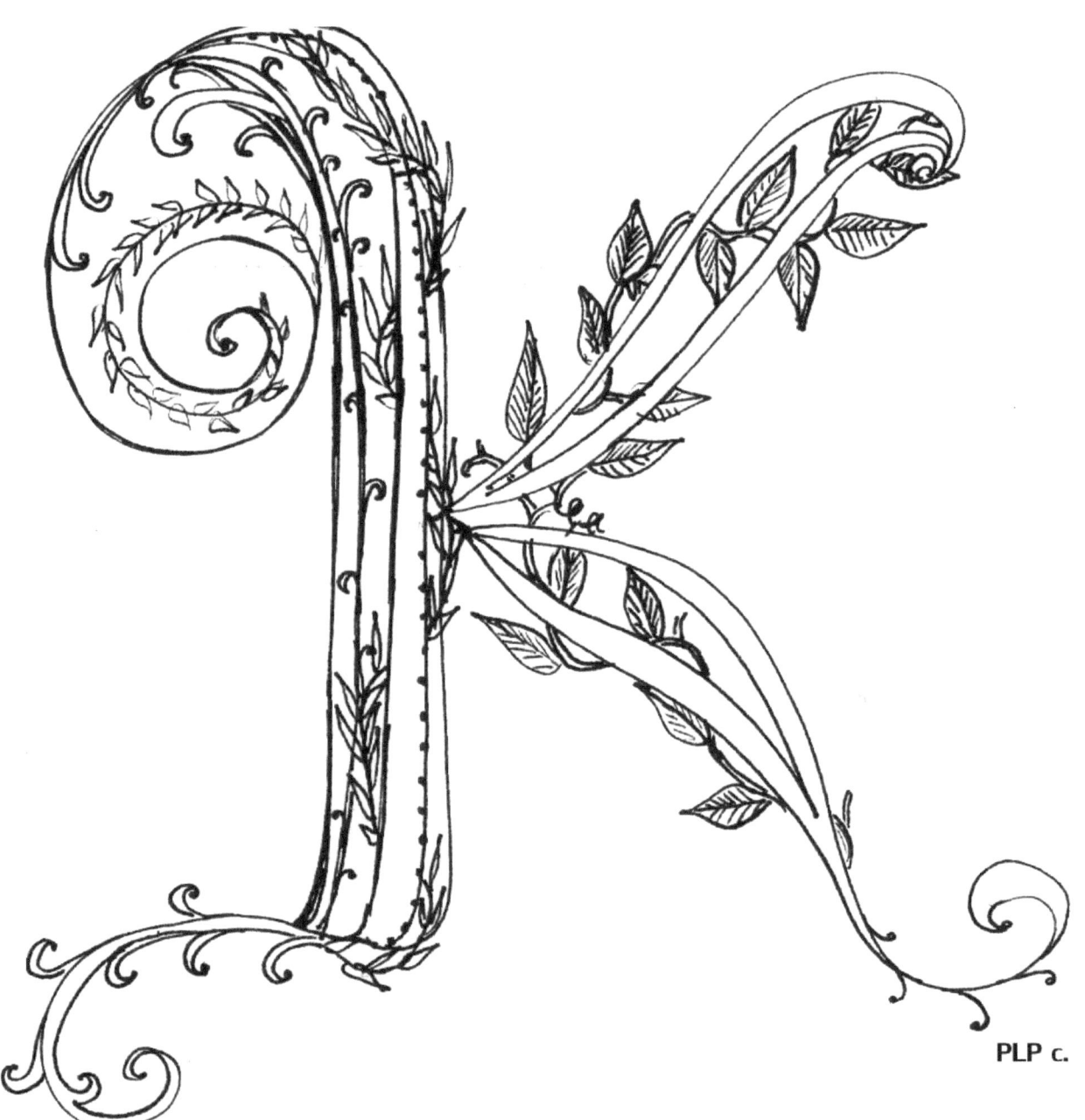

PLP c.

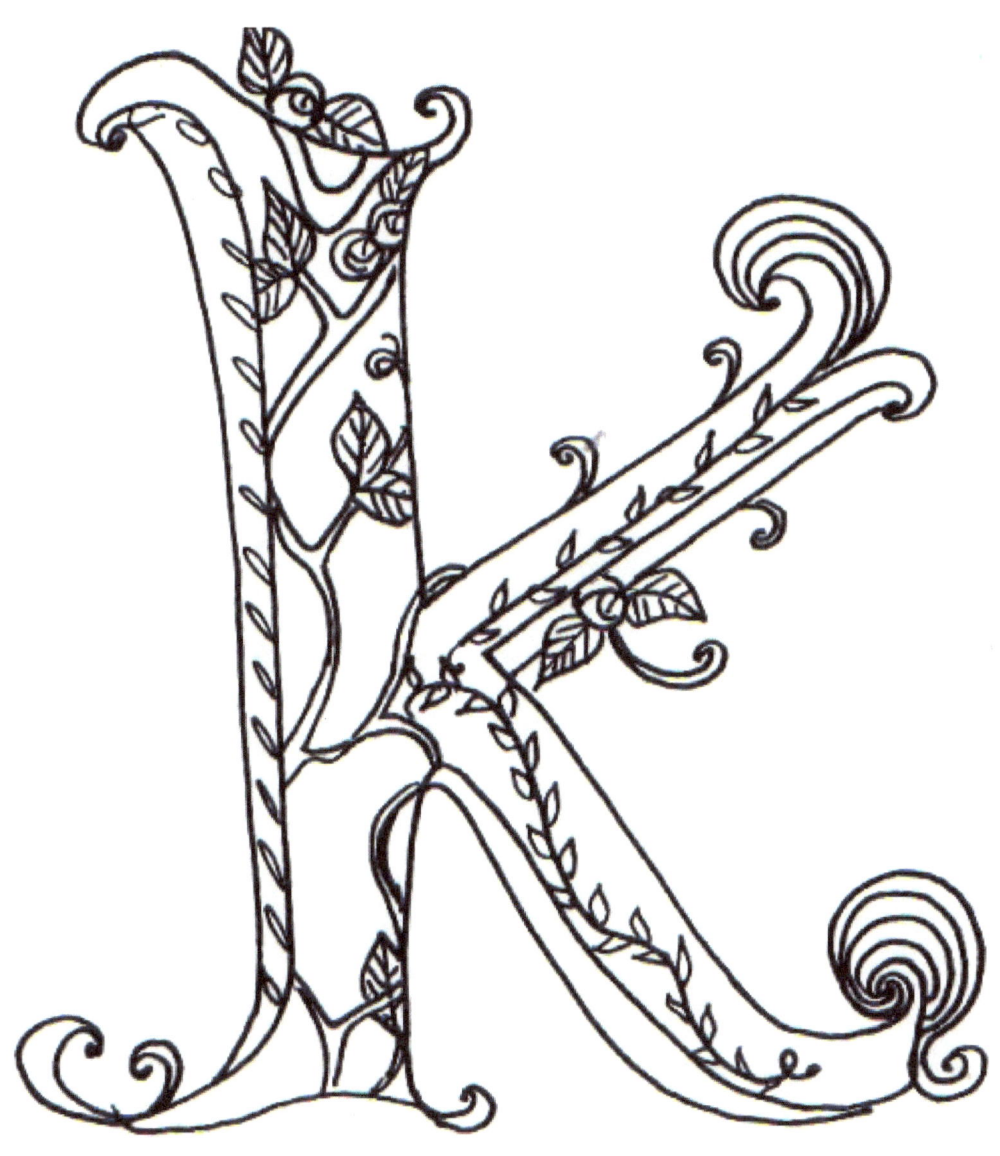

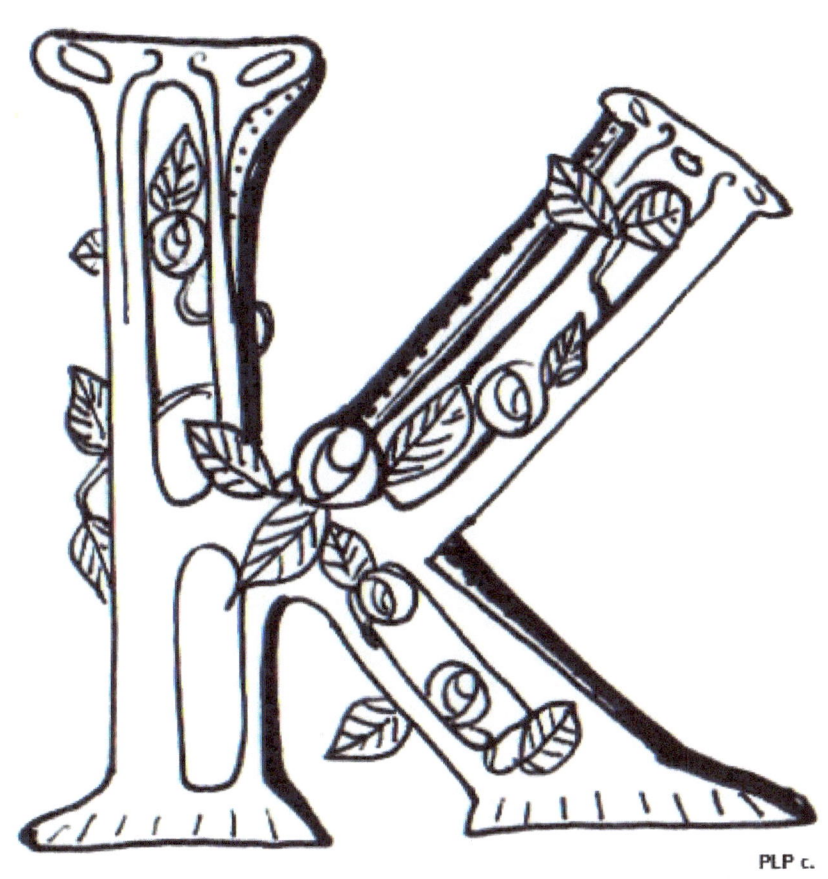

PLP c.

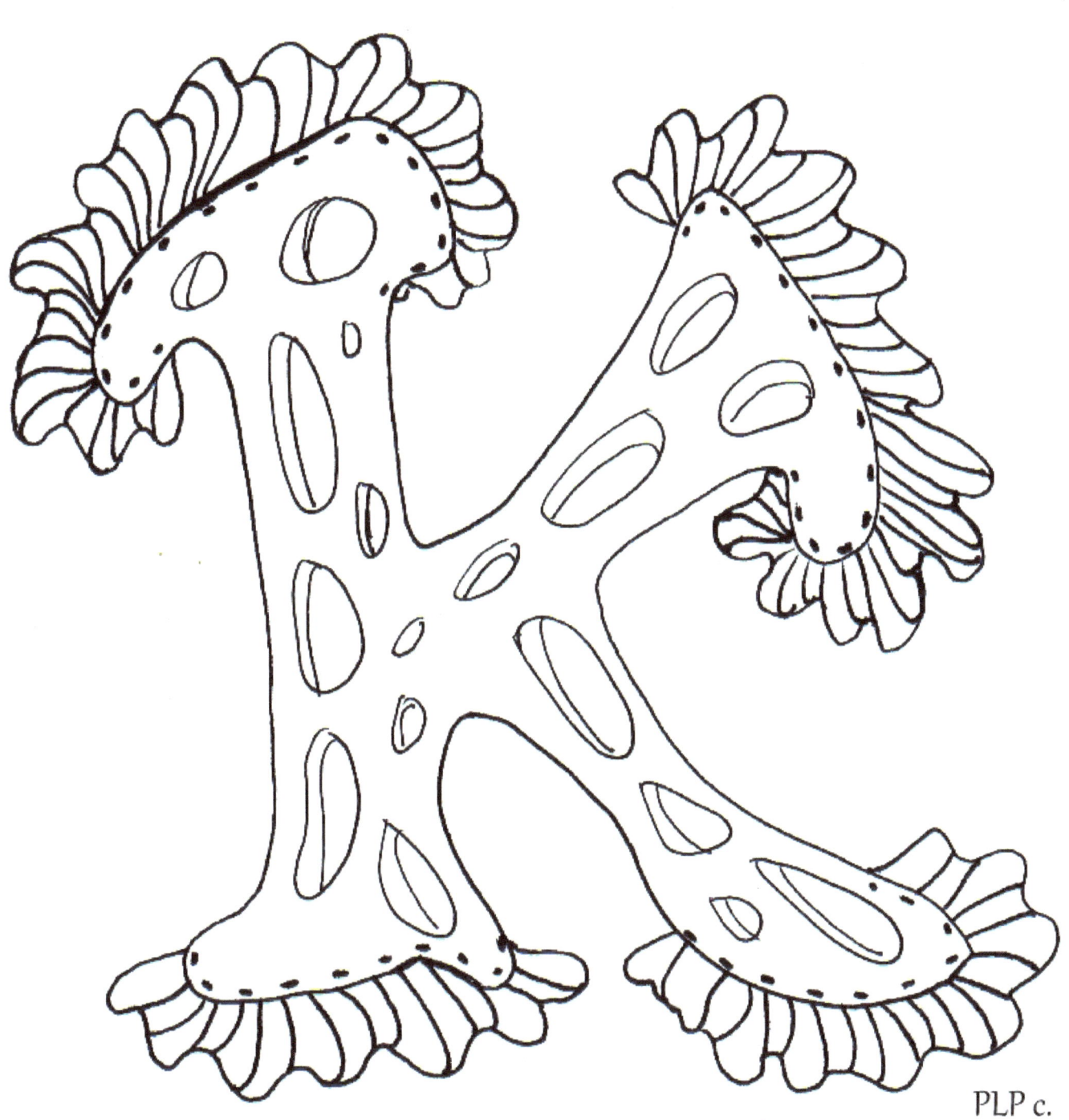

PLP c.

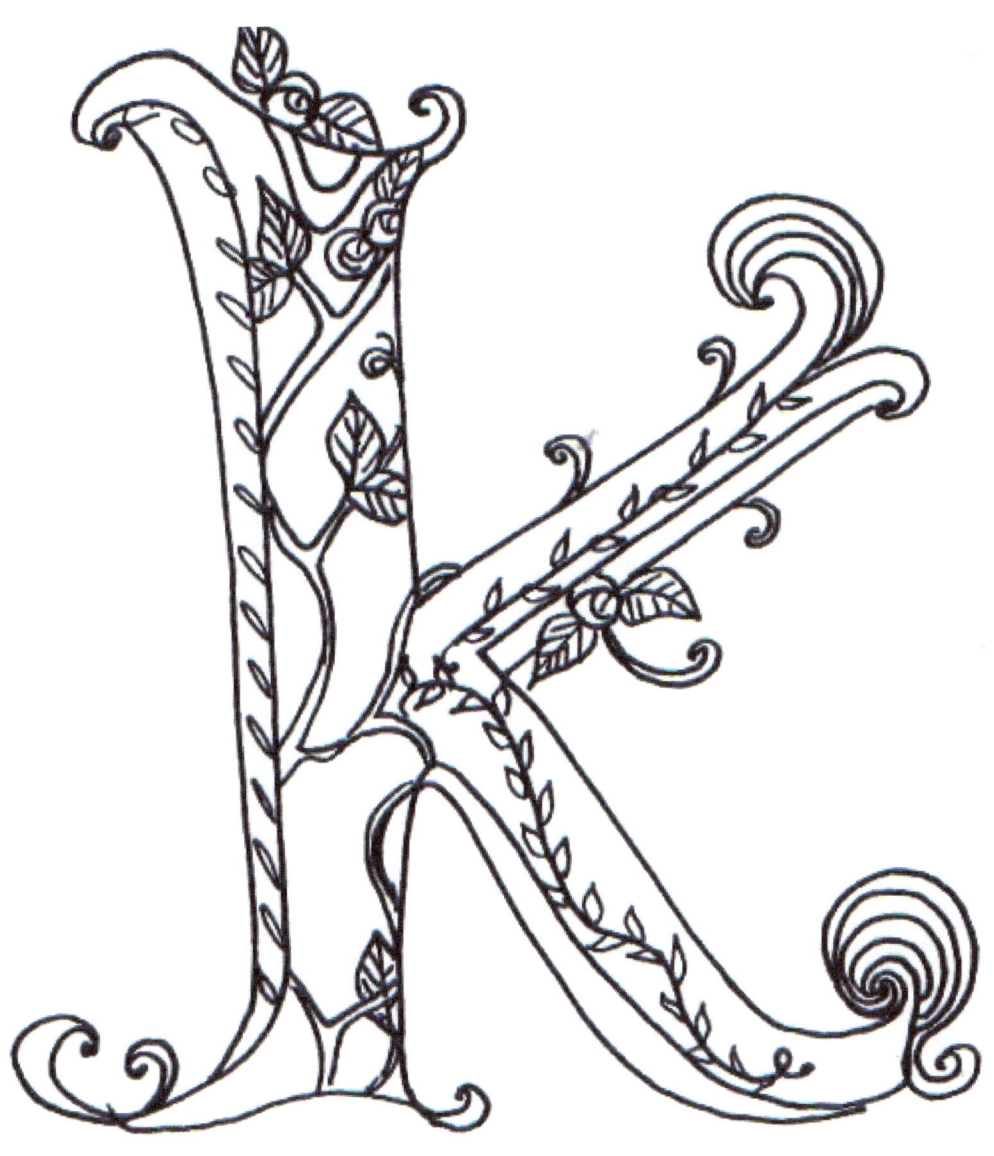

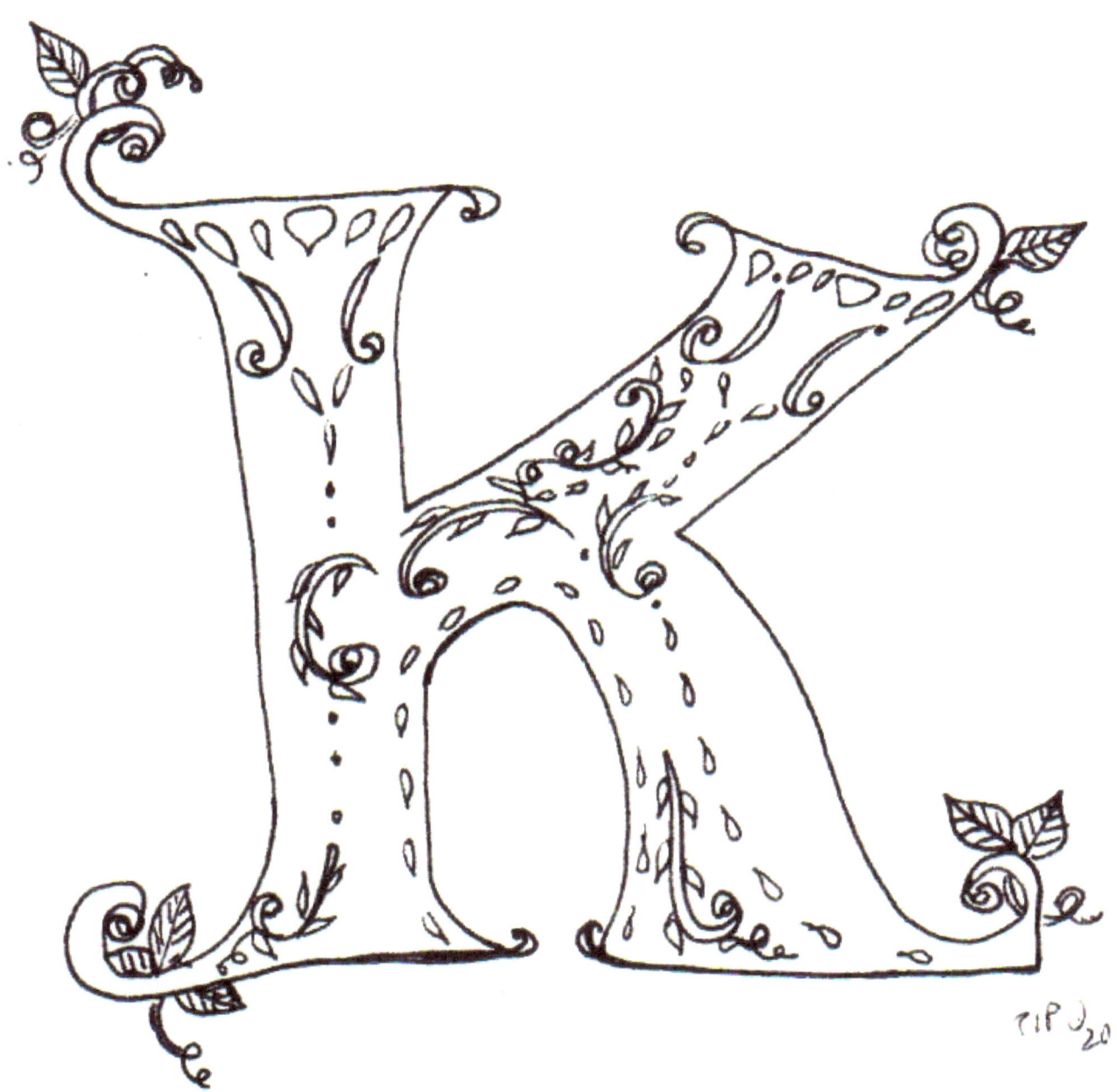

49

COWBOY "K"

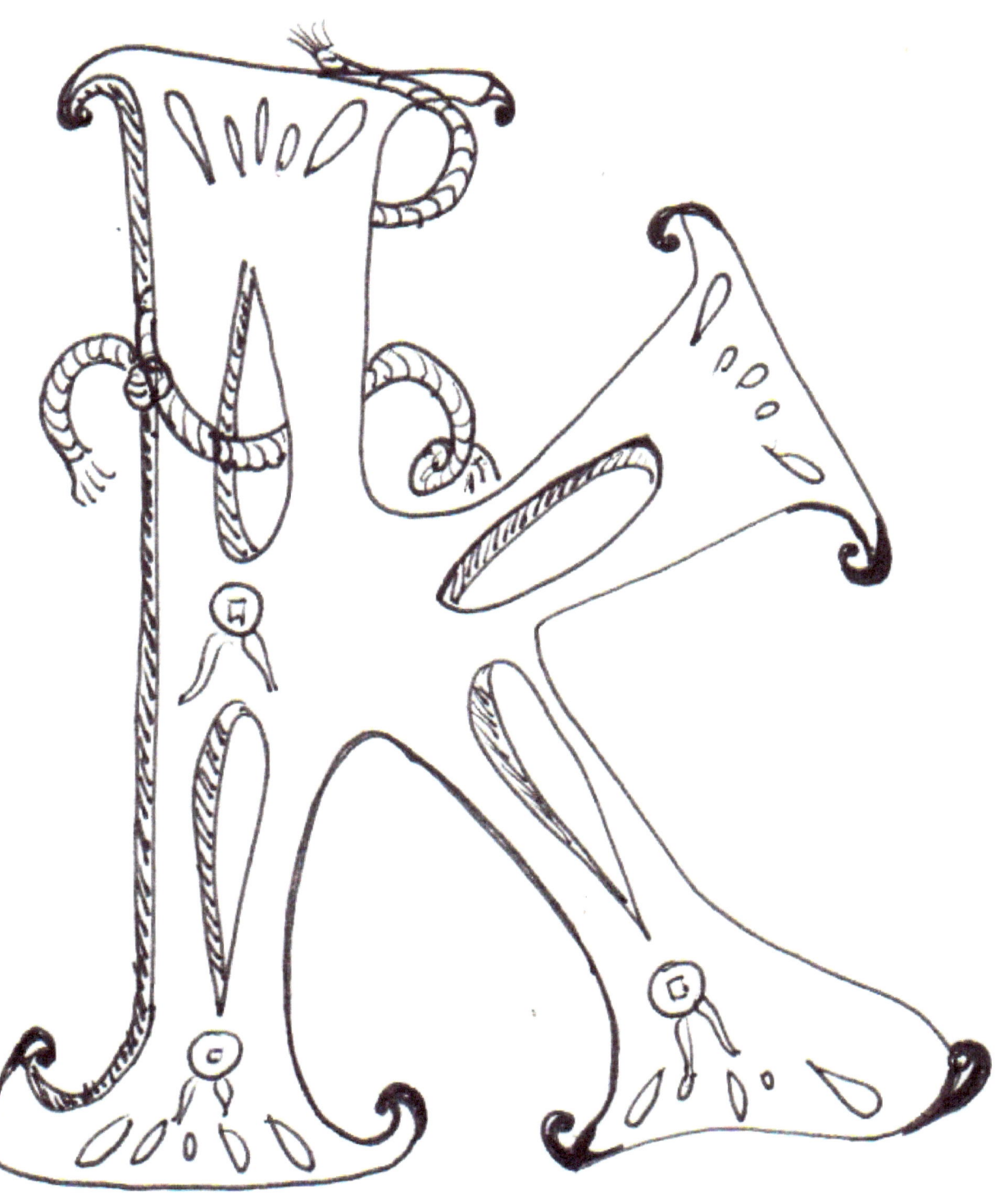

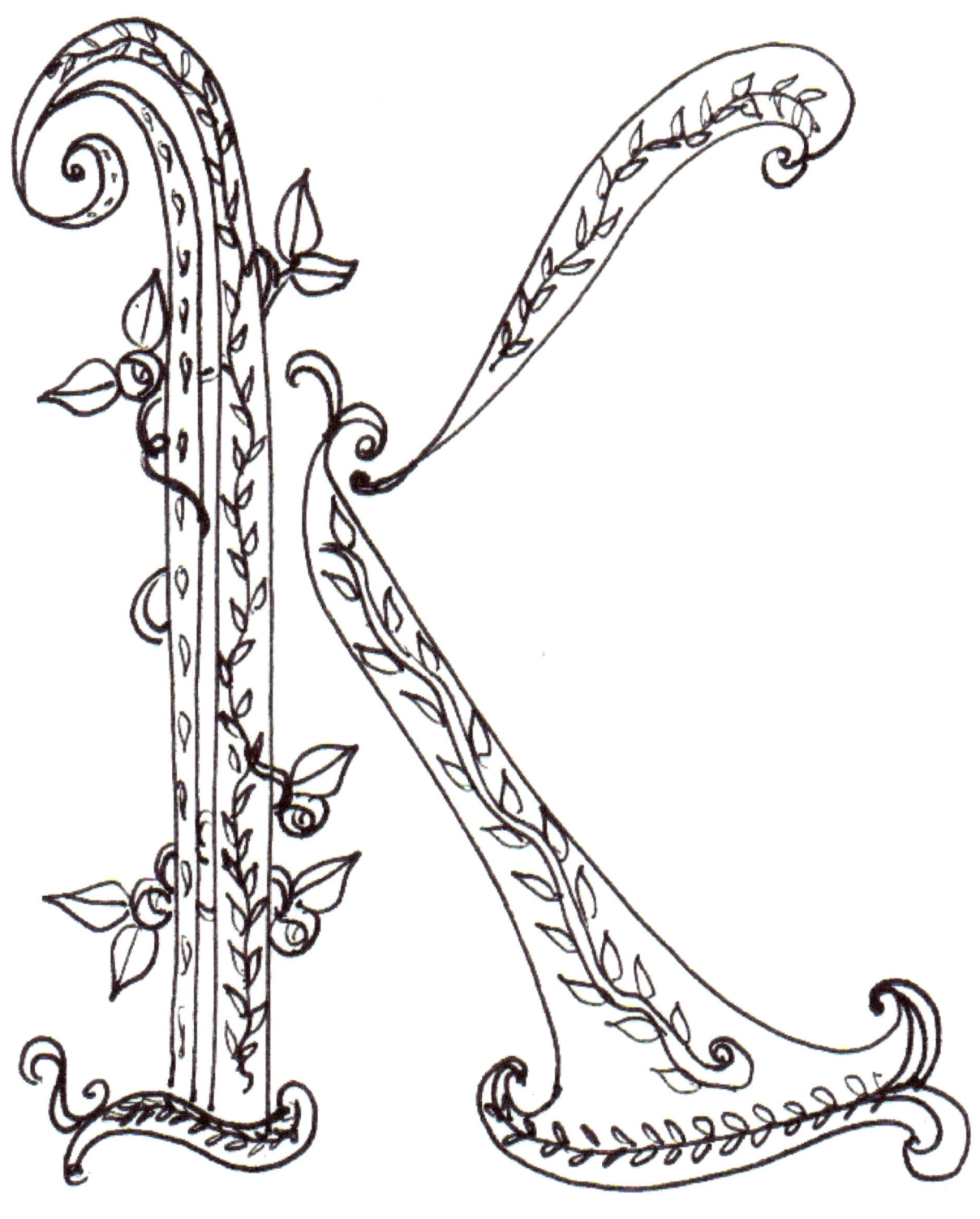

PLP c.

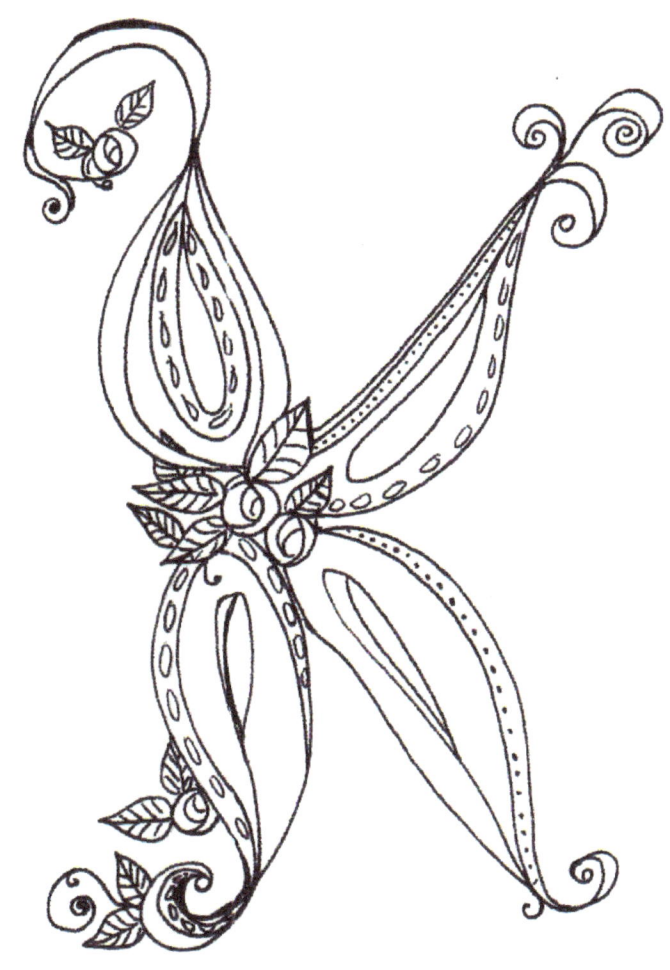

Letter "K"

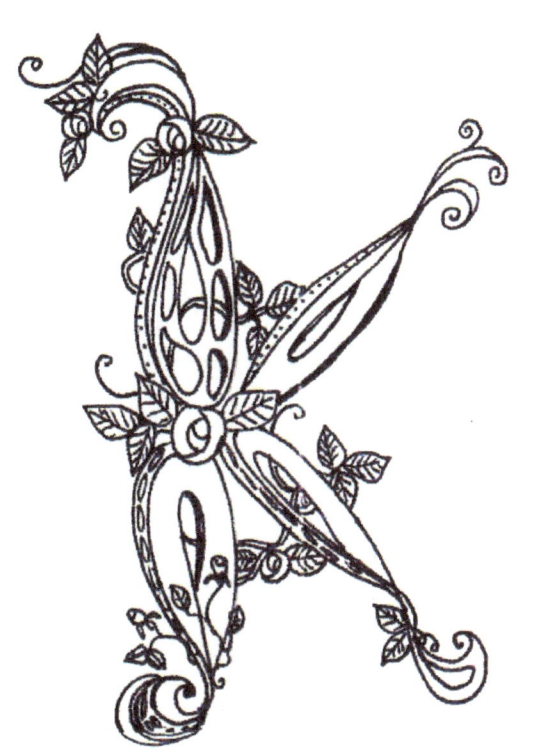

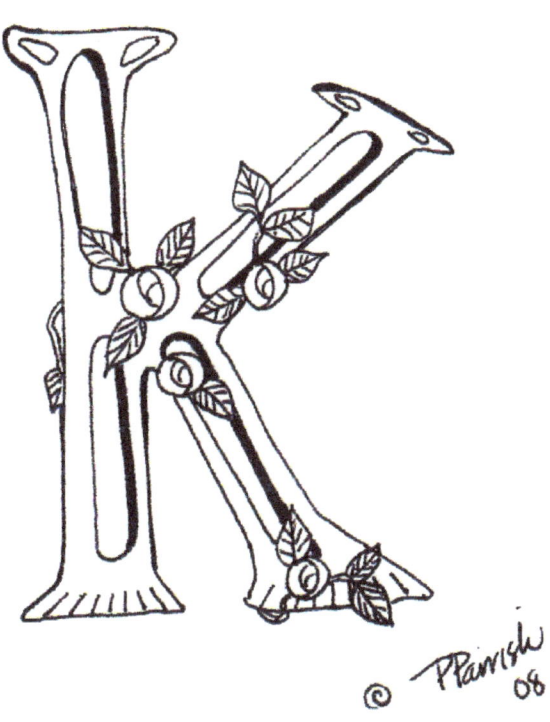

© P.Parrish 08

55

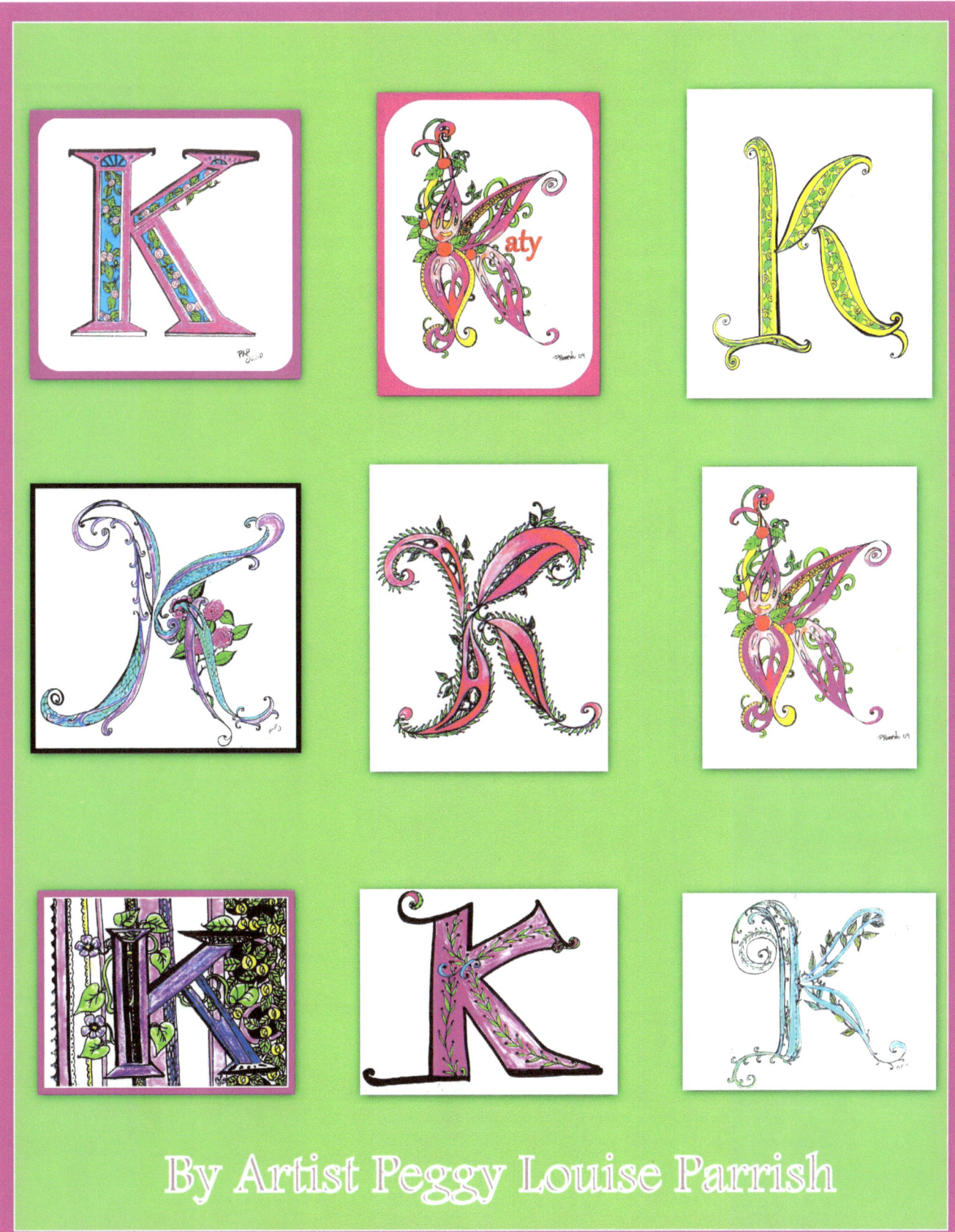

By Artist Peggy Louise Parrish

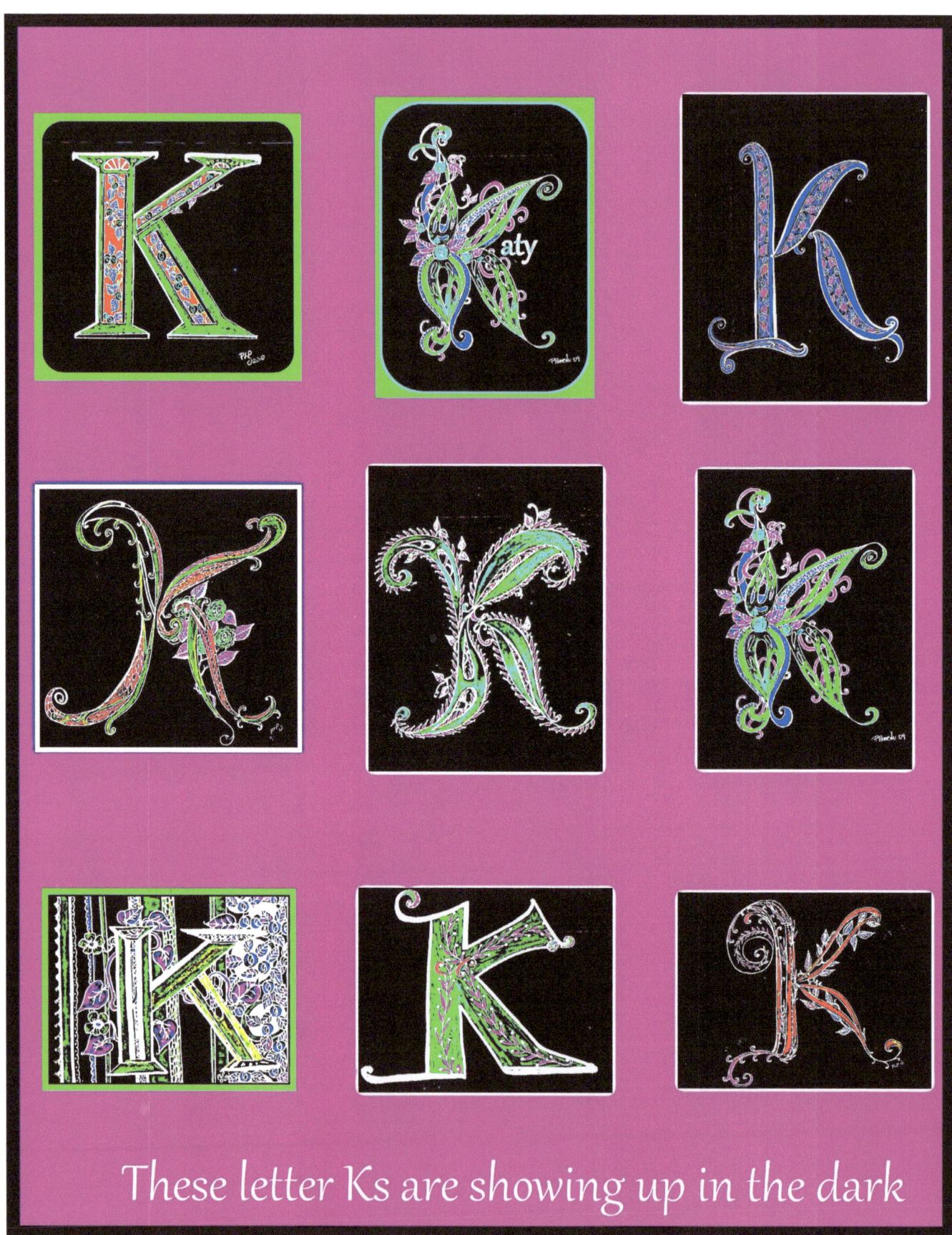

These letter Ks are showing up in the dark

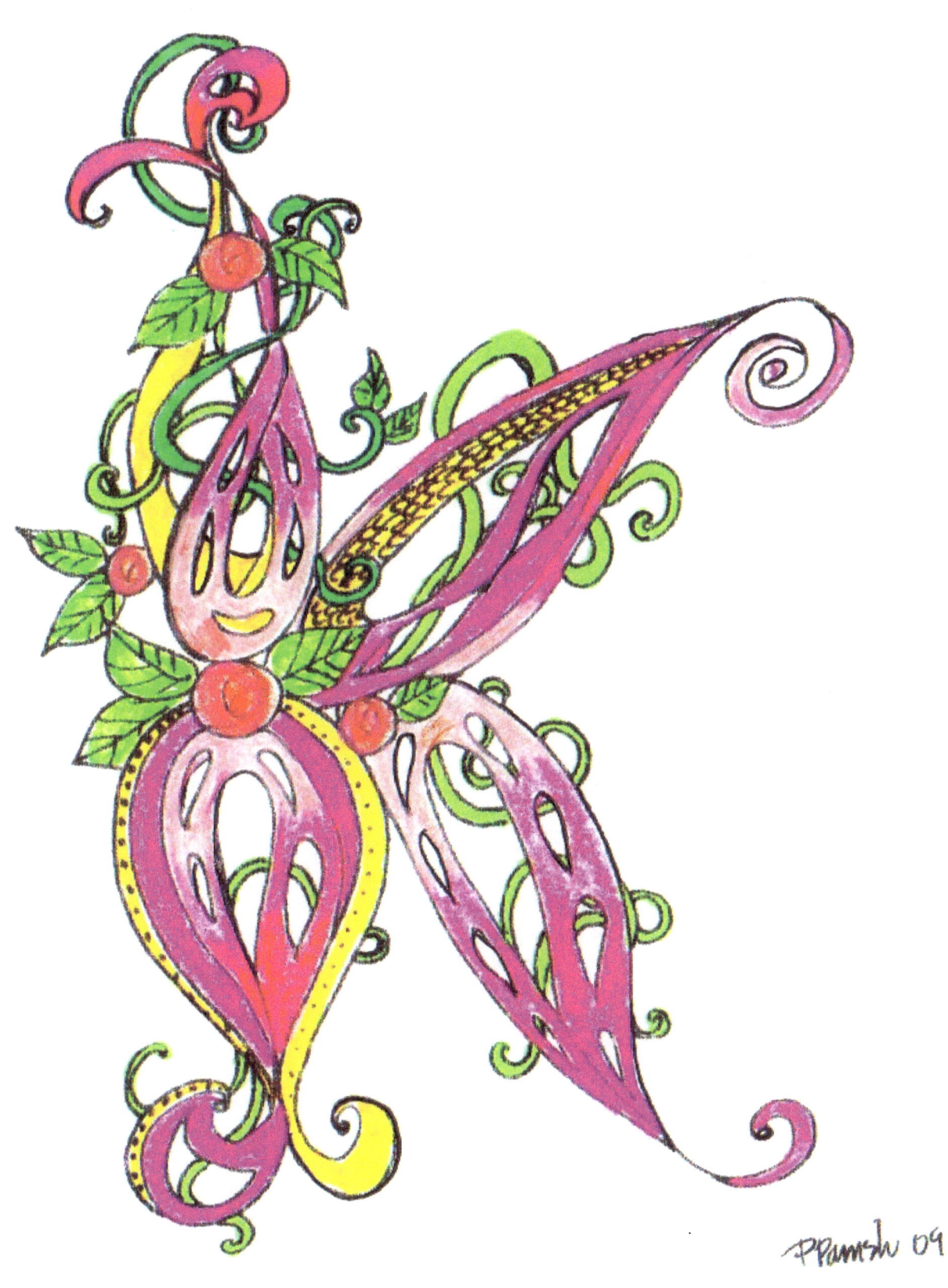

Have you ever thought of putting hearts in a letter? This letter K looks cute. What do you think?

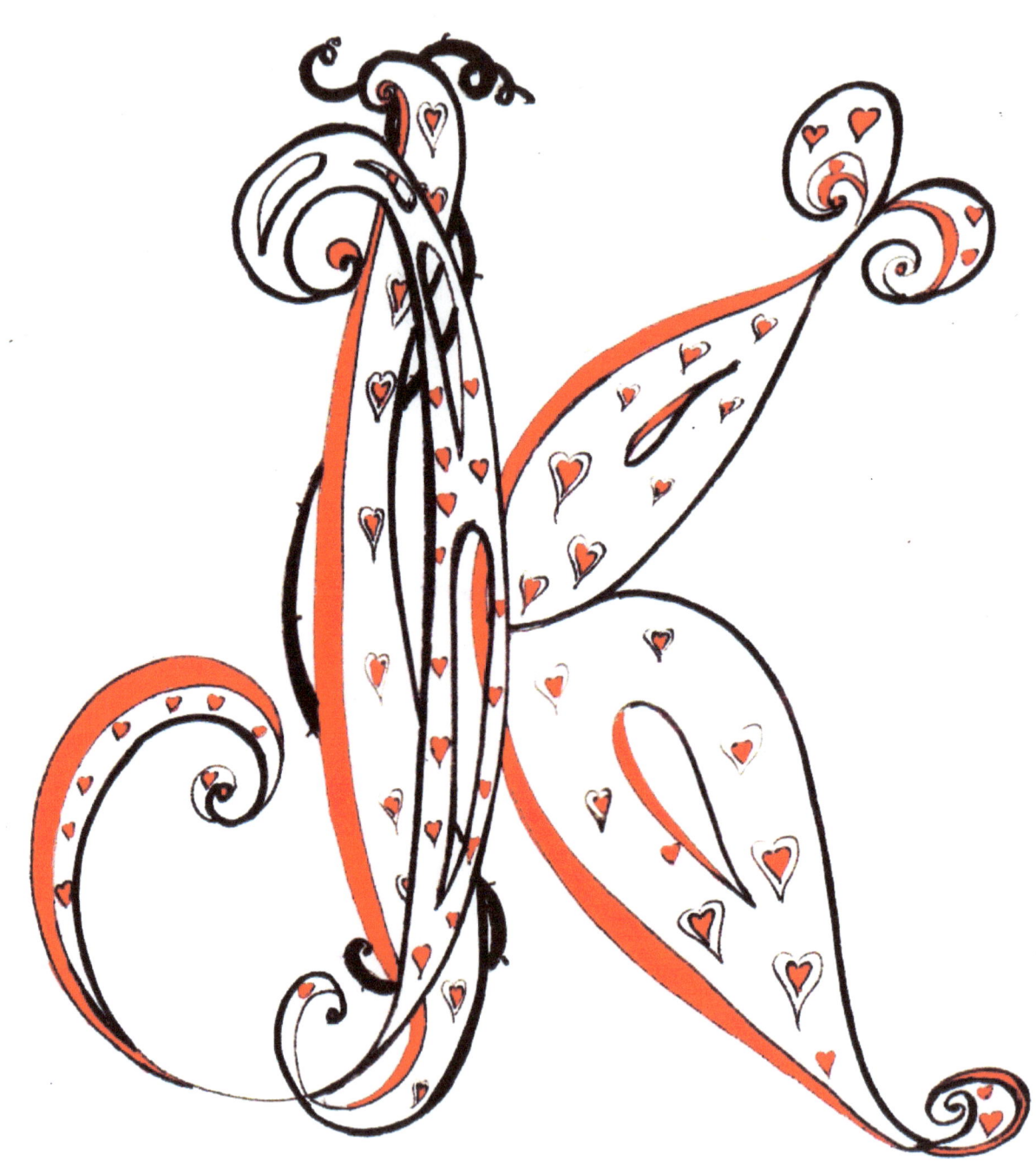

This K is enjoying the Wallpaper effect. Did you find the black and white of this K in this book?

Letter K can be surrounded by beauty!

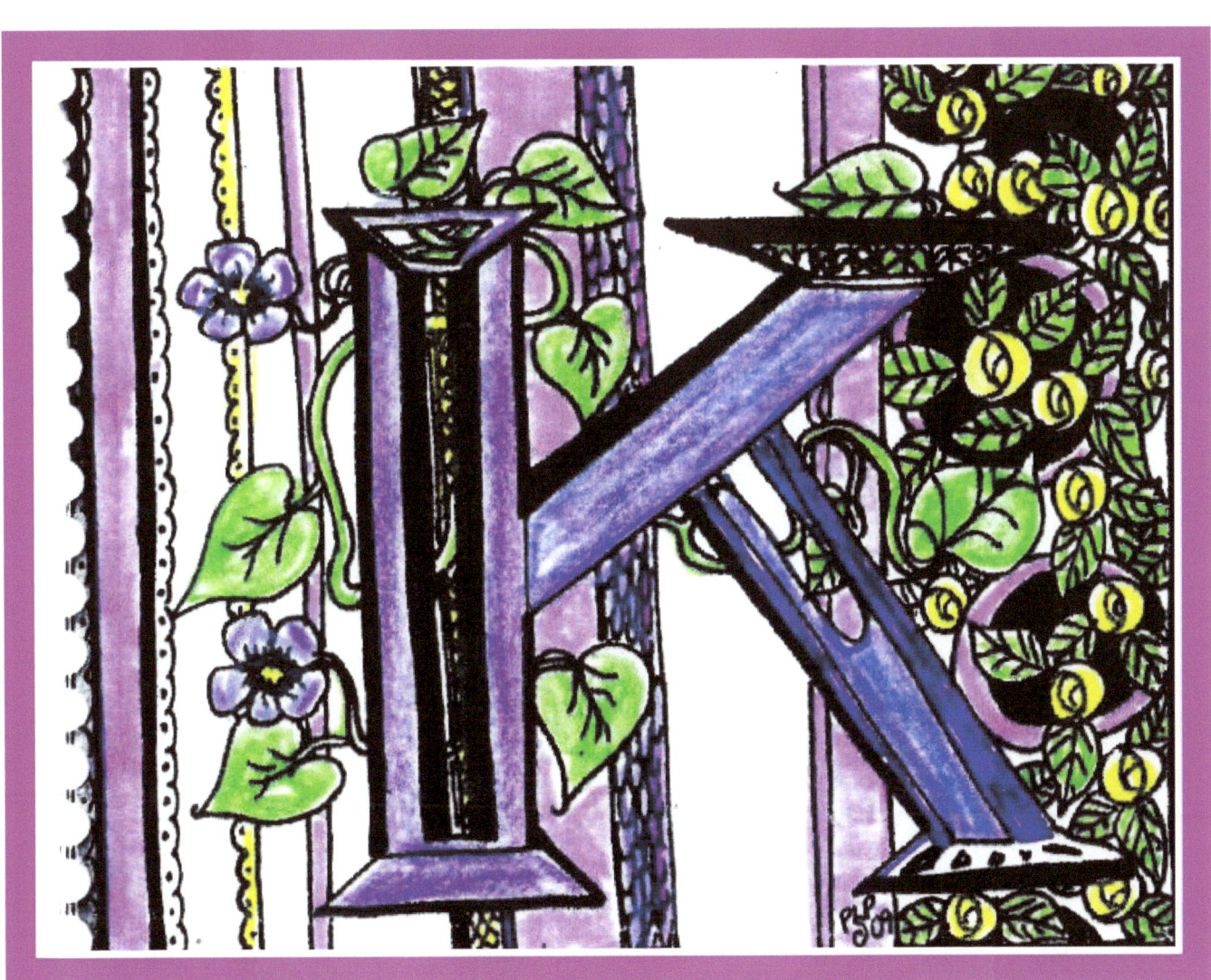

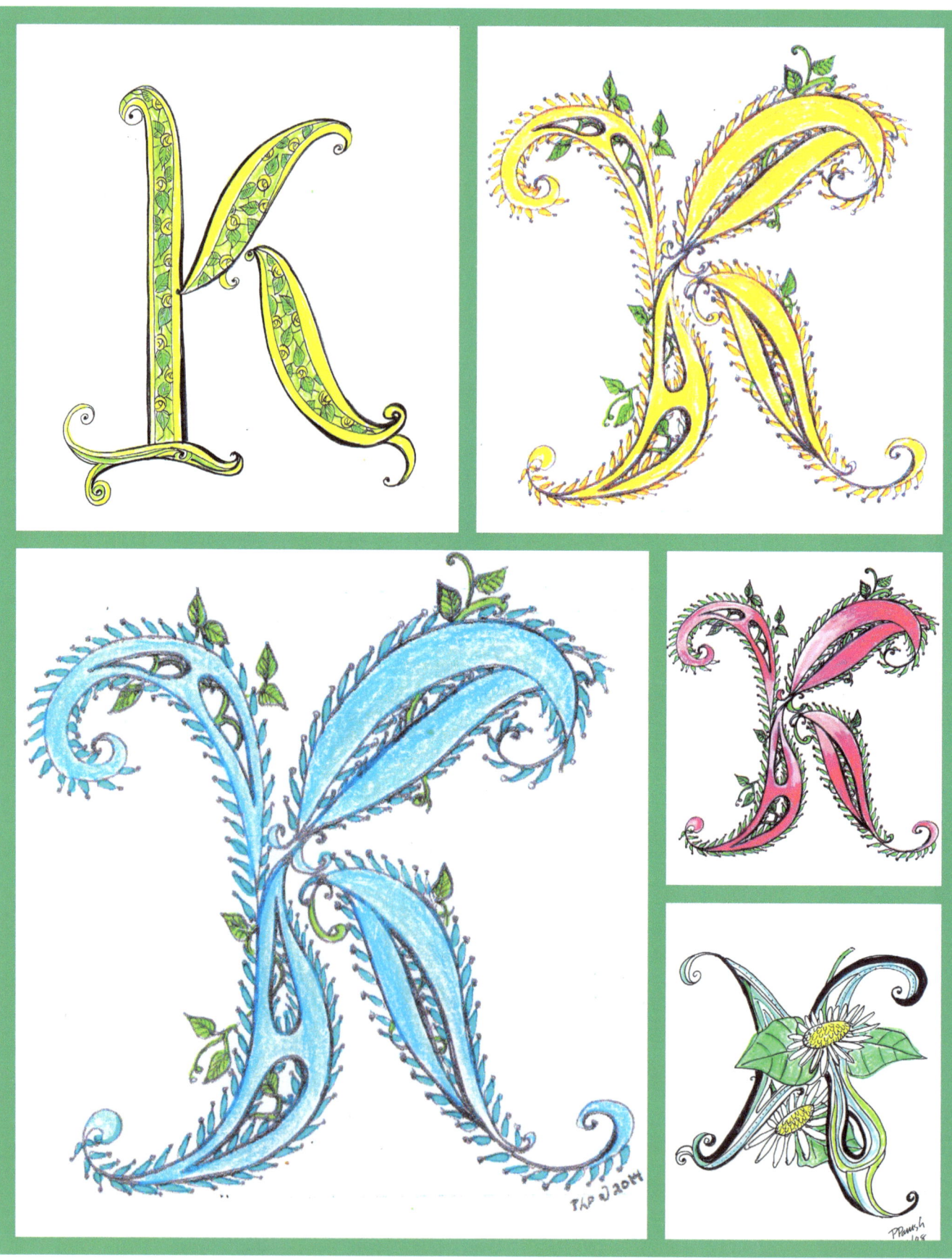

Are you having fun with letter K?

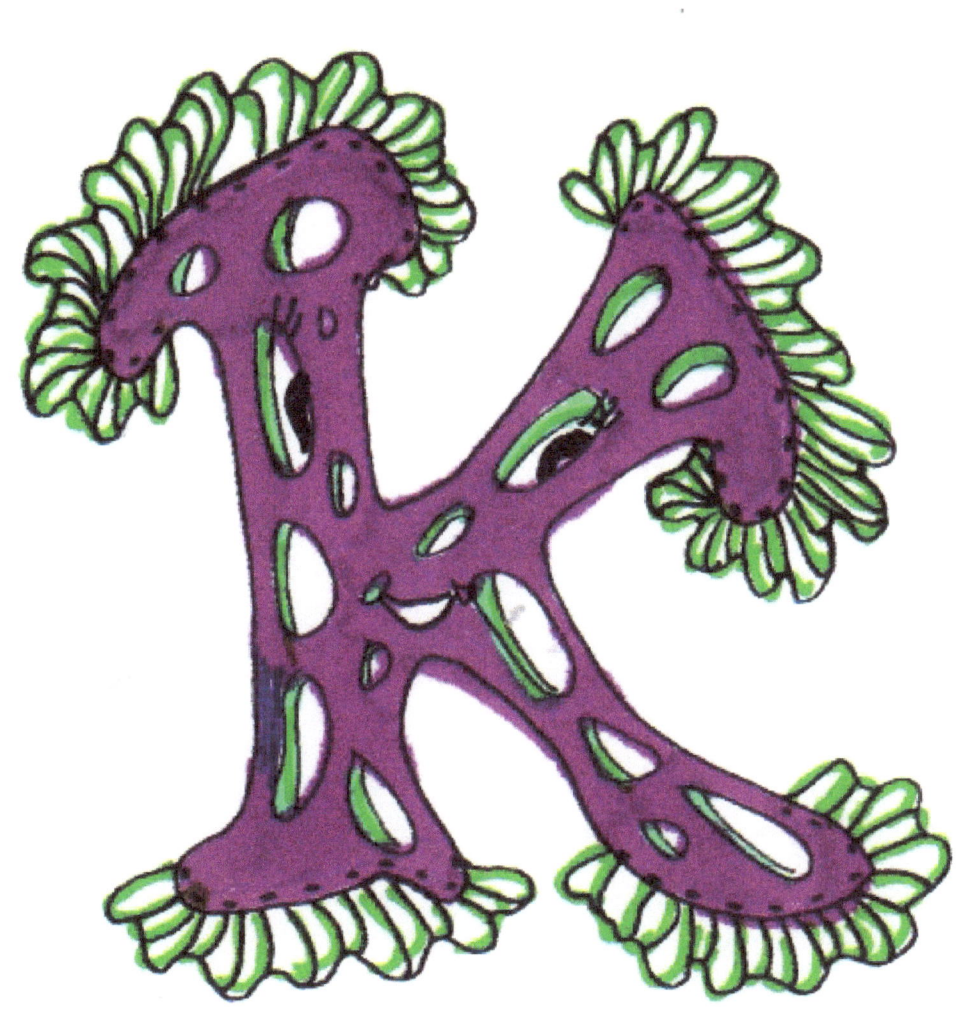

What kind of Letter K can you draw and color?